FOCUS ON ENDANGERED SPECIES
ENDANGERED MAMMALS

by Tammy Gagne

San Diego, CA

© 2024 BrightPoint Press
an imprint of ReferencePoint Press, Inc.
Printed in the United States

For more information, contact:
BrightPoint Press
PO Box 27779
San Diego, CA 92198
www.BrightPointPress.com

ALL RIGHTS RESERVED.

No part of this work covered by the copyright hereon may be reproduced or used in any form or by any means—graphic, electronic, or mechanical, including photocopying, recording, taping, web distribution, or information storage retrieval systems—without the written permission of the publisher.

LIBRARY OF CONGRESS CATALOGING-IN-PUBLICATION DATA

Names: Gagne, Tammy, author.
Title: Endangered mammals / by Tammy Gagne.
Description: San Diego, CA: BrightPoint Press, [2024] | Series: Focus on endangered species | Includes bibliographical references and index. | Audience: Ages 13 | Audience: Grades 7-9
Identifiers: LCCN 2023004139 (print) | LCCN 2023004140 (eBook) | ISBN 9781678206468 (hardcover) | ISBN 9781678206475 (eBook)
Subjects: LCSH: Rare mammals--Juvenile literature. | Endangered species--Juvenile literature.
Classification: LCC QL706.8 .G34 2024 (print) | LCC QL706.8 (eBook) | DDC 599.168--dc23/eng/20230316
LC record available at https://lccn.loc.gov/2023004139
LC eBook record available at https://lccn.loc.gov/2023004140

CONTENTS

AT A GLANCE	4
INTRODUCTION FIGHTING FOR SURVIVAL	6
CHAPTER ONE RED WOLVES	12
CHAPTER TWO AMUR LEOPARDS	20
CHAPTER THREE MOUNTAIN GORILLAS	34
CHAPTER FOUR BLACK RHINOS	46
Glossary	58
Source Notes	59
For Further Research	60
Index	62
Image Credits	63
About the Author	64

AT A GLANCE

- Human activities such as industrialization, deforestation, and poaching have caused many animals to become endangered.

- Red wolves are the most endangered wolves in the world. Their population was destroyed by habitat loss, loss of prey, and poaching. They went extinct in the wild in 1980.

- Scientists saved the red wolf by breeding the species in captivity. Although red wolf numbers have risen, they are still endangered.

- The Amur leopard is threatened by deforestation, loss of prey, and poaching. Many people hunt them for their spotted coats.

- Hundreds of thousands of acres have been turned into protected areas for Amur leopards. Conservationists are also supplying the big cats with prey. The leopards' population is slowly increasing.

- Mountain gorillas are endangered due to deforestation, climate change, and poaching.

- Conservationists are working with African communities to end poaching and deforestation. They are also using tourism to teach people about gorillas.

- Black rhinoceroses have become endangered because of poachers. These people kill rhinos and sell their horns. The horns are often ground into powder and used in medicines.

- Conservationists have had to get creative about ways to save black rhinos. They have even considered allowing a small number of people to hunt the animals legally.

INTRODUCTION

FIGHTING FOR SURVIVAL

The July sun rises as a red wolf closes in on a white-tailed deer. The wolf is tired after tracking the animal for hours. Hunting is difficult in the summer. It takes a lot of energy to cover so much ground in the heat. Food can be hard to find at this time of year. Prey such as this deer can hide easily among the leaves.

The wolf springs toward a bush. But it chooses the wrong one. The deer uses the

Red wolves are carnivores, but they sometimes eat insects and berries.

opportunity to dart away. It leaps out of the brush and disappears into the trees.

The wolf chases the deer for only a few yards before it gives up. Following the deer any farther is pointless. The wolf has reached the edge of the forest. Buildings stand where trees once grew. Some of the wolf's pack members have been hit by cars speeding along the nearby road. Some people have shot wolves in this area. This wolf's mate was killed by meat poisoned by humans.

The wolf catches a new scent. It's a raccoon. It doesn't notice the wolf. The wolf

Red wolves have few natural predators, but humans may drive them to extinction.

catches and eats the raccoon. The wolf might not survive tomorrow. But today it can rest with a full stomach.

As of 2023, 27 percent of mammal species were at risk of extinction.

HOW DO ANIMALS BECOME ENDANGERED?

Red wolves are endangered. This means their population is dangerously low.

Some people are trying to save the red wolf. But it will likely go extinct if more isn't done to protect the species. Many other **mammal** species are facing similar fates.

Animals can become endangered for many reasons. Overhunting, disease, and **habitat** loss all cause animal populations to decrease. Humans are responsible for many of these problems. But they can also be part of the solution. With education and effort, people can save endangered species from extinction.

1
RED WOLVES

The red wolf's fur is mostly brown or tan with some black along its back. The species is named for the reddish fur behind its ears, on its muzzle, and on the backs of its legs. Most red wolves are about 4 feet (1.2 m) long. They usually weigh between 45 and 80 pounds (20–36 kg).

Red wolves are social creatures. They spend their entire lives with one partner. Most red wolf packs are led by a mated pair. Their offspring make up the rest of the pack. A red wolf litter can range from a single pup to as many as nine young wolves.

Red wolf families work together. Older red wolves help raise their younger siblings.

Red wolves may hunt as a pack or alone. The animals will cover great distances while hunting. Some red wolves have been known to travel up to 20 miles (32 km) in search of prey. They hunt deer and raccoons. They also hunt small mammals such as rabbits and rodents.

DRIVEN TO EXTINCTION

Red wolves were once found throughout the southeastern United States. Their range stretched from Texas to Pennsylvania. Sometimes they were seen as far north as New York. Red wolf populations dropped as human populations grew. Humans killed the wolves for sport. Red wolf habitats were destroyed to build houses and farms. Their prey disappeared with the land.

By the early 1900s, red wolves were found only in Texas and Louisiana. The United States declared the species

SUSPICIOUS SPECIES

Some biologists didn't think red wolves were a real species. They thought red wolves came from gray wolves mating with coyotes. But in 2019, a study by the National Academy of Sciences proved that the red wolf was its own species. This meant it was able to receive endangered species protections.

endangered in 1973. The US Fish and Wildlife Service was worried that the wolves would disappear. John Dorsett was one of the biologists who worked to save the wolves. He says conservationists eventually decided that "the best bet [for saving the species] would be a captive breeding program."[1] Scientists began capturing as many red wolves as they could find. Biologists were able to breed fourteen of the seventeen red wolves that were captured. But this left no known red wolves in the wild. In 1980, the United States declared the species extinct in the wild.

Though hunted by humans who fear for their livestock, red wolves protect farms by killing pests.

SAVING THE RED WOLVES

The breeding program kept the species alive in **captivity**. Eventually, biologists began releasing some red wolves into the wild in North Carolina. Breeding programs now exist around the country. Scientists use radio collars to keep track of the released animals.

By 2006, the number of wild red wolves had risen to 130. But populations soon began decreasing again. The animals' endangered status made them illegal to kill. But some people kept hunting them. By 2021, there were about 250 wolves in

THE COYOTE PROBLEM

Coyotes pose a big risk to red wolf populations. Red wolves must breed with other red wolves to survive as a unique species. But sometimes they breed with coyotes instead. Some biologists **sterilize** coyotes that live near red wolves. This prevents hybrids from being born.

captive breeding programs. But there were only ten collared wolves in the wild.

By 2023, the red wolf had become the most endangered wolf species in the world. But conservationists continued to do everything they could to save these animals. In 2022, six wolf pups were born in the wild at Alligator River National Wildlife Refuge in North Carolina. It was the first time a wild litter had been born in four years. Both the mother and the father were also born in the wild. The litter offers some hope that the species may survive.

2
AMUR LEOPARDS

The Amur leopard has a paler coat than most leopard species. Its light-yellow base often turns reddish yellow in the winter. The coat is spotted with dark **rosettes**.

An Amur leopard's size can vary greatly. A small female can weigh just 55 pounds (25 kg). But a large male can weigh up to 105 pounds (48 kg). These strong cats are remarkably agile. They can jump up to 10 feet (3 m) into the air. Some have

The spots on Amur leopard coats are as unique as fingerprints. They can be used to tell leopards apart.

been seen leaping up to 19 feet (5.8 m) forward. They can run at up to 37 miles per hour (60 kmh).

Amur leopards spend most of their lives alone. But males seek out females during mating season. This takes place in January and February. Male cats will often fight over females. Many male Amur leopards will go back to living alone after mating with a female cat. But some males stay to help raise their young. Cubs usually drink their mother's milk until they're around three months of age. They stay with their mother until they are about two years old.

Amur leopards usually give birth to two or three cubs at a time. Cubs don't open their eyes until they're a week old.

Amur leopards are carnivores. Their diet is made up mainly of deer and boars. When this larger prey isn't available, leopards will settle for rabbits or mice. Amur leopards do not like to share their kills with other predators. They will sometimes drag a kill up a tree to keep other animals from stealing it.

SURVIVING IN THE WILD

Amur leopards live farther north than any other large-cat species. They are found in the forests of eastern Russia and northeastern China. The cats were named after the nearby Amur River.

Most large cats live in warmer regions. But the Amur leopard is **adapted** to its colder climate. The cat's heavy coat keeps the animal warm. Its thick fur can grow

Amur leopards have huge paws. This lets them walk on snow without sinking.

nearly 3 inches (7.6 cm) long during the winter. The light color helps the animal blend in with the snow. Its rosettes are also spaced more widely apart than those of other leopards. This design helps the cat remain hidden while hunting.

Amur leopards have few predators. But they sometimes fight with tigers over prey. This happens when food is hard to find. Tigers often win these battles.

The leopard's small range also makes disease a big risk. An illness could spread through the population quickly. Big cat vet John Lewis explains, "If you have diseases

DANGERS OF DISTEMPER

In 2015, a sick Amur leopard was found on a roadside in Russia. Vets found that she had distemper. This virus usually attacks dogs. But it has also been found in certain tiger species. If distemper strikes more Amur leopards, it could wipe out the remaining wild population.

going through the leopard prey species, diseases like foot and mouth or swine fever, and if you get a bad outbreak of either of those diseases, you will lose leopards."[2]

ENDANGERED LEOPARDS

Humans have taken over land where Amur leopards once lived. Farms, logging camps, railways, and fuel pipelines have replaced their territory. The Amur leopard lost about 80 percent of its habitat between 1970 and 1983.

Forest fires have also reduced the leopards' habitat. As the land recovers from

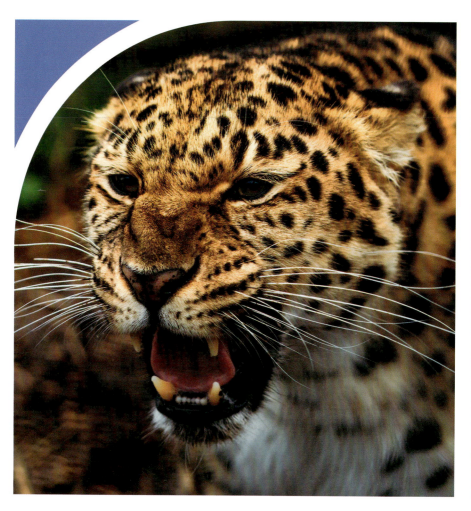

Poachers kill Amur leopards for their pelts. Poachers can get up to $1,000 for a single pelt.

these disasters, grasslands grow in place of the forests. Amur leopards prefer not to live in these open spaces. Catching prey is difficult for the large cat when other animals can see it coming. Open spaces also expose the leopards to tigers.

Hunting also greatly decreased the leopard's population. Some hunters killed Amur leopards to sell the cats' spotted fur. Other hunters killed Amur leopards to get rid of hunting competition. These people hunted deer and boars to feed their own families. But the Amur leopards often got to the prey before human hunters could.

When the Amur leopard became endangered, governments outlawed hunting the cats. But **poachers** continued killing them. The leopards' shrinking range made it easier for poachers to find and kill the cats.

The Amur leopard's numbers dropped even further over the next few decades. By the mid-2000s, experts estimated that fewer than forty of the leopards remained in the wild. Pavel Fomenko worked for the World Wildlife Fund (WWF) at this time. In 2007, he said, "The predator is on the brink of extinction."[3]

The population has increased slowly since this all-time low. Scientists now think there are about one hundred Amur leopards

Amur leopards are active mostly at night. Scientists have to use night-vision cameras to monitor them.

living in the wild. About 70 percent of their range falls within protected areas. This means that people cannot develop the land. Russia is a big part of this effort. The country set aside 650,000 acres (263,000 ha) of land to protect

Amur leopards. This protected area is called Land of the Leopard National Park. In 2017, a research center opened in the park. This will let scientists study how to best protect this endangered species. In addition to giving leopards more land, Russia is also giving harsh punishments to poachers. Conservationists hope these efforts will help the Amur leopard population keep growing.

The WWF is also working to save these big cats. Less land means less prey. The WWF combats this problem by putting extra prey such as deer and wild boars in Amur leopard habitats.

The Amur leopard population is beginning to recover. In 2022, fourteen Amur leopard babies were born in Land of the Leopard National Park.

3
MOUNTAIN GORILLAS

Mountain gorillas are among the smartest animals in the world. Researchers have seen this species using natural objects as tools. Mountain gorillas in captivity have even learned to communicate using sign language. Mountain gorillas have large heads and muscular arms.

They lean forward on their arms to walk. Female mountain gorillas can weigh up to 215 pounds (98 kg). Males are usually much larger. They can reach 484 pounds (220 kg).

Long hair covers most of the mountain gorilla's body. It can vary from black

Wild mountain gorillas live for about thirty-five years.

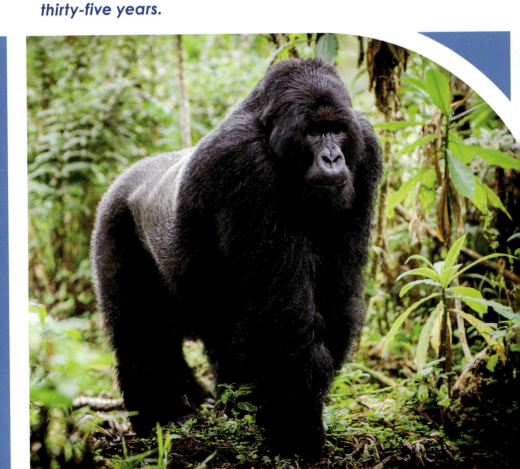

to grayish brown in female gorillas and younger males. Males turn silverly gray when they reach adulthood. These adult males are called silverbacks.

Mountain gorillas live in groups called troops. Troops normally include about ten gorillas. One silverback serves as the leader of each troop. The leader decides when the troop eats and rests.

Most of the mountain gorillas' diet is made up of leaves, shoots, and stems. They also eat fruits, wild celery, tree bark, and insects.

Adult male mountain gorillas eat up to 75 pounds (34 kg) of food every day.

Mountain gorillas are generally calm animals. Members of a troop usually get along well. But the top silverback will become aggressive if challenged by another gorilla. He may pound his chest, throw

Each gorilla troop has a territory of up to 16 square miles (41 sq km).

things, or charge toward the other gorilla to prove that he is the most powerful animal.

GORILLAS IN DANGER

Mountain gorillas are named after their natural habitat. The species lives in the mountains of east-central Africa. About half of its population is found in the Virunga mountains of Uganda, Rwanda, and the Democratic Republic of the Congo. Others live in Uganda's Bwindi Impenetrable National Park.

Temperatures in mountainous regions can drop below freezing. This is not an issue for mountain gorillas. Their hair is longer and thicker than that of other great apes. It keeps them warm when the weather is cold. When it gets warmer, mountain gorillas rest in shady parts of the forest to cool down.

Gorillas sleep in nests made of leaves. Mother gorillas sleep with their babies to keep them warm in the cold climate.

High temperatures can create a problem for the species. Mountain gorillas get most of their water from the plants they eat.

But the gorillas still need some drinking water. The amount they need increases with warmer temperatures.

Unfortunately, **climate change** is causing temperatures to rise. This makes the apes need more water. But water isn't always nearby. Mountain gorillas may soon need to travel beyond their natural range to find more water. This movement could take them away from their food sources.

Journalist Joshua Rapp Learn explains, "If temperatures get consistently hotter due to climate change, the combination of having to find standing water and having to hide deep in vegetation to rest could take away from foraging."[4] He adds that it could also create a dangerous cycle. Eating less would give the gorillas less energy to search for food. This cycle could make it hard for the species to thrive.

THE THREAT OF COVID-19

National parks where mountain gorillas live temporarily shut down to visitors in 2020 due to the COVID-19 pandemic. Not even researchers were allowed to enter. Gorillas can catch many illnesses from humans. Scientists worried that a COVID-19 outbreak could devastate the wild mountain gorilla population.

LOSING THEIR HOMES

German soldier Robert von Beringe identified the mountain gorilla as a new species in 1902. Scientists soon warned that the animals' future was in danger. People started moving into the regions where the gorillas lived. They cut down the forests where the gorillas foraged. Some people even hunted the gorillas for meat.

By the late 1960s, only a few hundred mountain gorillas were left in the wild. A scientist named Dian Fossey wanted to save the mountain gorilla. In 1967, she founded a research center in Rwanda.

She spent most of the next two decades living in the forests and studying gorillas. By 1981, she reported that there were only 254 mountain gorillas left. She felt strongly that people were the gorillas' biggest problem. She hired people to destroy animal traps and protect the gorillas from poachers.

Fossey didn't think that people should interact with gorillas. She thought this would disturb them. But other conservationists believed that education and tourism were the best ways to save the mountain gorillas. They encouraged people to visit Rwanda and see the gorillas in person. The conservationists thought this would help people care more about the mountain gorilla. This strategy worked. Mountain gorilla numbers have grown. By 2022, there were about 1,000 mountain gorillas living in the wild.

GUARDING GORILLAS

After Fossey's death in 1985, the organization she founded continued. Today the Dian Fossey Gorilla Fund trains conservationists and works with local communities to help gorillas. The organization gets rid of animal traps, protects gorillas from poachers, and stops people from cutting down trees in the gorillas' habitat.

4
BLACK RHINOS

Black rhinos can stand up to 6 feet (1.8 m) tall and weigh up to 3,080 pounds (1,400 kg). A black rhino has two horns on the top of its nose. The horns can grow as much as 3 inches (7.6 cm) in a year. The slightly longer front horn usually measures about 1.5 feet (0.5 m). But some reach a length of 5 feet (1.5 m).

Rolling in mud keeps away bugs and stops the rhinos from getting sunburned.

The black rhinoceros isn't actually black. It's gray. Its name might come from one of its favorite pastimes. Black rhinos often lie in mud to stay cool. Their bodies become covered in dark mud. This makes them appear darker than they are.

This huge animal is among the most endangered species in the world. Some people kill these rhinos for sport. Others kill the rhinos for their horns. Some people believe that rhino horns make powerful medicine when ground into powder. They use the medicine to try to cure a variety of health problems such as fever and cancer.

There is no scientific evidence that rhino horns help with any medical condition. But poachers kill the animals anyway. They can get thousands of dollars for a single horn. In 2020, journalist Kara Jamie Norton reported, "The horn is so valuable it can be sold on the black market for three times the price of gold."[5]

OTHER RHINOS IN DANGER

Four of the rhinoceros species in the world today are at risk of extinction. In addition to the black rhino, the Javan rhino, the northern white rhino, and the Sumatran rhino are critically endangered. The western black rhino has already gone extinct.

Black rhinos use their horns for many purposes. Horns help rhinos defend themselves when other animals threaten their territory. Mother rhinos use their horns to protect their young from predators. They also use them to guide their offspring. Horns are especially useful for finding food and water. Rhinos use their horns to break branches off trees. They also use them to dig for water.

THE BLACK RHINO'S HABITAT

Most black rhinos live in southern Africa. As much as 87 percent of the population is

Black rhino calves stay with their mothers for about three years.

found in Kenya, Namibia, and South Africa. Most black rhinos live in protected reserves where hunting is not allowed.

Black rhinoceroses can survive in a variety of environments. They can live in grasslands, woodlands, forests, or wetlands. Black rhinos are herbivores. They eat many different plants. This allows them to find food in any of their environments. Rhinos are browsers. This means that they move around while feeding on the available vegetation.

Baby rhinos are called calves. These young animals sometimes become the prey of hungry lions or hyenas. But adult rhinos have no predators other than humans.

CREATIVE CONSERVATION

Humans have nearly driven the black rhinoceros extinct. The wild black rhino

Almost 200 black rhinos live in zoos.

population dropped 98 percent between 1960 and 1995. Fewer than 2,500 were left in the wild. Conservationists began working hard to save the species. They made protected areas where black rhinos can roam. But poachers are still a constant threat.

It is illegal to hunt most black rhinos. But poachers take the risk because of the money they can make from rhino horns. This problem has forced many conservationists to get creative about protections. Some people think that allowing a very small amount of hunting could save the species. Some hunters are willing to pay large sums for permits to hunt rhinos. This money could then be used for conservation.

Namibia is one country that is working to protect black rhinos. About 20 percent of the country is reserved for wildlife refuges.

Some people think the best way to prevent poaching is by removing horns from the rhinos. This makes the animals less valuable to poachers. But there are problems with this idea. Conservationist Dereck Joubert is against horn removal. He points out that rhinos need their horns. He also argues that some poachers would kill a black rhino for just the small amount of horn that remains. He says, "That's why baby rhinos are also being killed now, just for the nub. . . . The answer is not in dehorning them, but in protecting and in stopping the illegal trade."[6]

Saving endangered mammals is a big job. The steps that must be taken are different for each species. But by working together, governments and conservationists

WHERE IN THE WORLD?

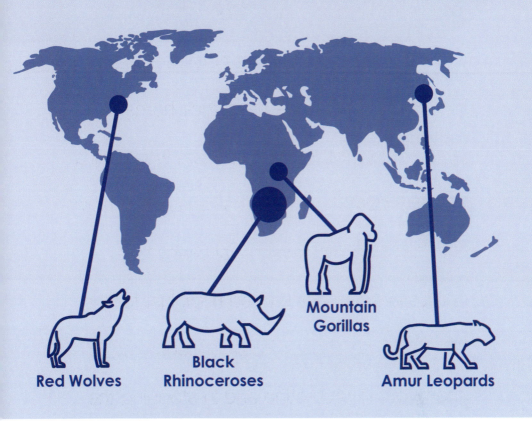

Endangered mammals live around the world. However, without further protections, they might disappear completely.

can keep today's endangered animals from

going extinct in the future.

GLOSSARY

adapted

adjusted to one's environment

captivity

the state of being confined

climate change

the process of the world getting hotter due to human activity such as pollution

habitat

the place where a plant or animal normally grows or lives

mammal

an animal that makes milk to feed its young

poachers

people who kill or capture animals illegally

rosettes

spots shaped like roses

sterilize

to remove sex organs to prevent offspring

SOURCE NOTES

CHAPTER ONE: RED WOLVES

1. Quoted in David Todd, "The Last Few Wolves," *Texas Fauna Project*, June 14, 2021. www.texasfauna.org.

CHAPTER TWO: AMUR LEOPARDS

2. Quoted in Wildlife Vets, "An Interview with Dr. John Lewis," *Wildlife Vets International*, July 12, 2018. www.wildlifevetsinternational.org.

3. Quoted in Rhett Butler, "Less than 35 Amur Leopards Remain in the Wild," *Mongabay*, April 19, 2007. https://news.mongabay.com.

CHAPTER THREE: MOUNTAIN GORILLAS

4. Joshua Rapp Learn, "Climate Change Is Making Mountain Gorillas Thirstier," *Discover*, April 14, 2022. www.discovermagazine.com.

CHAPTER FOUR: BLACK RHINOS

5. Kara Jamie Norton, "The Pandemic's Effect on Wildlife: An Interview with National Geographic Photographer and Filmmaker Ami Vitale," *PBS Nature*, May 11, 2020. www.pbs.org.

6. Quoted in Bret Love, "Interview: Dereck Joubert," *Green Global Travel*, n.d. https://greenglobaltravel.com.

FOR FURTHER RESEARCH

BOOKS

Tim Cooke, *Return to Yellowstone: Gray Wolf Comeback*. Minneapolis, MN: Bearport Publishing, 2022.

Clara MacCarald, *Endangered Whales*. San Diego, CA: BrightPoint Press, 2024.

Sandra Markle, *The Great Rhino Rescue: Saving the Southern White Rhinos*. Minneapolis, MN: Millbrook Press, 2019.

INTERNET SOURCES

"Gorillas," *DK Find Out!*, n.d. www.dkfindout.com.

"Leopards," *National Geographic*, n.d. www.nationalgeographic.com

"Rhinoceros," *San Diego Zoo*, n.d. https://animals.sandiegozoo.org.

WEBSITES

African Wildlife Federation
www.awf.org

The African Wildlife Federation works to protect wildlife in Africa. It practices African-led conservation to both protect the natural world and provide opportunities for the surrounding communities.

US Fish and Wildlife Service
www.fws.gov

The US Fish and Wildlife Service is a government agency. It works to conserve and manage fish, wildlife, plants, and the environment.

World Wildlife Fund
www.worldwildlife.org

Created in 1961, the World Wildlife Fund protects animals and their habitats. It works to conserve wildlife in almost 100 countries.

INDEX

Africa, 39, 50
Alligator River National Wildlife Refuge, 19
Amur leopards, 20–33, 57
Amur River, 24

black rhinos, 46–56, 57
breeding program, 16–19
Bwindi Impenetrable National Park, 39

China, 24
coyotes, 15, 18

deforestation, 8, 15, 27, 43, 45
Democratic Republic of the Congo, 39
diet, 6–9, 14, 23–24, 26, 28–29, 32, 36, 40–41, 50, 52
disease, 11, 26–27, 42

endangered species protections, 15

Fossey, Dian, 43–44, 45
fur, 12, 20, 24–25, 29

hair, 35–36, 39
horns, 46–47, 48–50, 54–56

Kenya, 51

Land of the Leopard National Park, 32
Louisiana, 15

mates, 8, 13, 22
mountain gorillas, 34–45, 57

Namibia, 51
New York, 14
North Carolina, 17, 19

offspring, 13, 22, 50, 52, 56
overhunting, 11, 15, 29, 43, 48

Pennsylvania, 14
poaching, 8, 18, 29–30, 32, 44, 45, 48–49, 54–56
population, 10–11, 14, 18–19, 29, 30, 39, 43–45, 50, 53

red wolves, 6–11, 12–19, 57
Russia, 24, 26, 31–32
Rwanda, 39, 43, 45

silverbacks, 36–37
size, 12, 20–21, 35, 46
South Africa, 51
speed, 22

Texas, 14–15
troops, 36–37

Uganda, 39
United States, 14–17
US Fish and Wildlife Service, 16

Virunga mountains, 39

World Wildlife Fund, 30, 32

62

IMAGE CREDITS

Cover: © Cathy Withers-Clarke/Shutterstock Images
5: © Warren Metcalf/Shutterstock Images
7: © Iftikhar Ahmad Khan/Shutterstock Images
9: © B. Bartel/NCTC Image Library/USFWS National Digital Library
10: © Richard Gray/iStockphoto
13: © Karen Crewe/Shutterstock Images
17: © B. Bartel/NCTC Image Library/USFWS National Digital Library
21: © Rachie B/Shutterstock Images
23: © Robert Franklin Photography/Shutterstock Images
25: © Gavin Baker Photography/Shutterstock Images
28: © BBA Photography/Shutterstock Images
31: © Mikhail Semenov/Shutterstock Images
33: © wrangel/iStockphoto
35: © Jurgen Vogt/Shutterstock Images
37: © Kiki Dohmeier/Shutterstock Images
38: © robertharding/Last Refuge/Alamy
40: © COULANGES/Shutterstock Images
47: © Lou Coetzer/Nature Picture Library/Alamy
51: © Lance van de Vyver/Shutterstock Images
53: © Sabine Heindorf/iStockphoto
55: © Shem Compion/Gallo Images/Alamy
57 (world map): © Irina Adamovich/Shutterstock Images
57 (rhino, gorilla, leopard): © karpenko_ilia/Shutterstock Images
57 (wolf): © Profi Trollka/Shutterstock Images

ABOUT THE AUTHOR

Tammy Gagne has written hundreds of books for both adults and children. Some of her favorite projects have been about endangered species and other animals. She lives in northern New England with her husband, son, and dogs.